Bunratty

Bunratty

Duncan Bruce Hose

PUNCHER & WATTMANN

First published in 2015
Published by Puncher and Wattmann
PO Box 441
Glebe NSW 2037
http://www.puncherandwattmann.com
puncherandwattmann@bigpond.com

National Library of Australia
Cataloguing-in-Publication entry:

Hose, Duncan Bruce
Bunratty

ISBN 9781922186881
I. Title.
A821.3

Cover design by Matthew Holt
Printed by McPherson's Printing Group

This project has been assisted by the Australian Government through the Australia Council, its arts funding and advisory body.

Australian Government

Australia Council
for the Arts

Contents

Liquor's not like that

Liquor's not lk that I said
        Digging in your skirt and learning thereby banjo
   I understocd the meaning of 'braves'
Only in my freedom t' fuck the whole world
 A great gnashing of britches

When   did   Tasmania   get   so
German   Anyway
Here we are in German Tasmania
Appeldorff   Little Alp,   hills are randy
w/ tearful horses,
                 Hohenzollern barns engineer the air to chasten

horny grasses\

Nostos (Excuse me)   Put me to charge
Nostoi (Excuse me)
Satan flying west a returning hero
 Soft as Titian and as tender, straight
          In to the lap of Saint Cherry Smythe.
Superb
       Fooling with the red painttube I spilt
Abit 'what co I do with is'? you lifted your shirt
  I fingerput a red rabbit on your furksome ladybelly

Menstrula; she's laying her labours down
That tought sits there on the painting table a soft pear
Rimbaud still stares out of Carjat's studio   at it seems me   Hello Arthur
Shall we make madrigal? You shitty little monarch

Two mill. Kilowatt muse we make carpet ahead of us with roughs of your hair
Sunday's shears- do nought but play me for the sounds of pleasure
Sex dough three split eggs carnal interview
Sherry Bee   my birthday bitch   my sunny church
                              Door my ticket booth attendant my warm
             Mouthpiece at the hopped telephone exchange

  joy-pellet
Be my peace of fruit flying at the bus window
       & Thrown of childe's hand
                        I don't require the form of you just
the atmosphere of turnpike
                                      Affection

Elvo New Yorko

Lust   the toothless whale-jaw
open up   /Horse thief O'Grady

Angelhair we

                                   Tickled New York and its glow-

    Worm assholes from above
Rue de St. Curse

                Rue de Ear Muff, aortas

      Flickering with terror, terror of
A cheerful mariachi band that follows you and won't quit like black
Balloons court in the birches on Bleecker Street

The greater achievement of the West   that   involved

                        Me at least
Was holding the C14th hand of the Madonna for a day at the Met.
We forgave each other that is

                      She didn't forgive me

Might I make a little tapenade

Of your spoils the bit of you I spoiled
Wake to find I have groomed myself to Death

(Balal, o fodder:--anoint, confound, X fade, mingle, mix (self), give
    provender, temper
The fig ripened at a pinch, that is ripened by pinching
Beelzebub)

I was swallowing

I was swallowing

  Iwasswallowing

  I was swallowing the coast

Sun comes on the swabbed   Deck as I

Sweare a circle around Manahatta

             Everything about a vessel is tension

                     These boards are bowed and so pact

United by thr. Desire to splinter

                 That's the check that keeps this

fucker together

         HMS Logarithm

              Later and lost In the streets of Harlem

w/ the seventy-proof pride of being   Grandly Drunk (we do these

   things alone)

               I think of Zelda Fitzgerald Facing up

        To the carpets in the foyer   of the Plaza Hotel

Hi , Zelda-in-pyjamas

might I share your snuff?

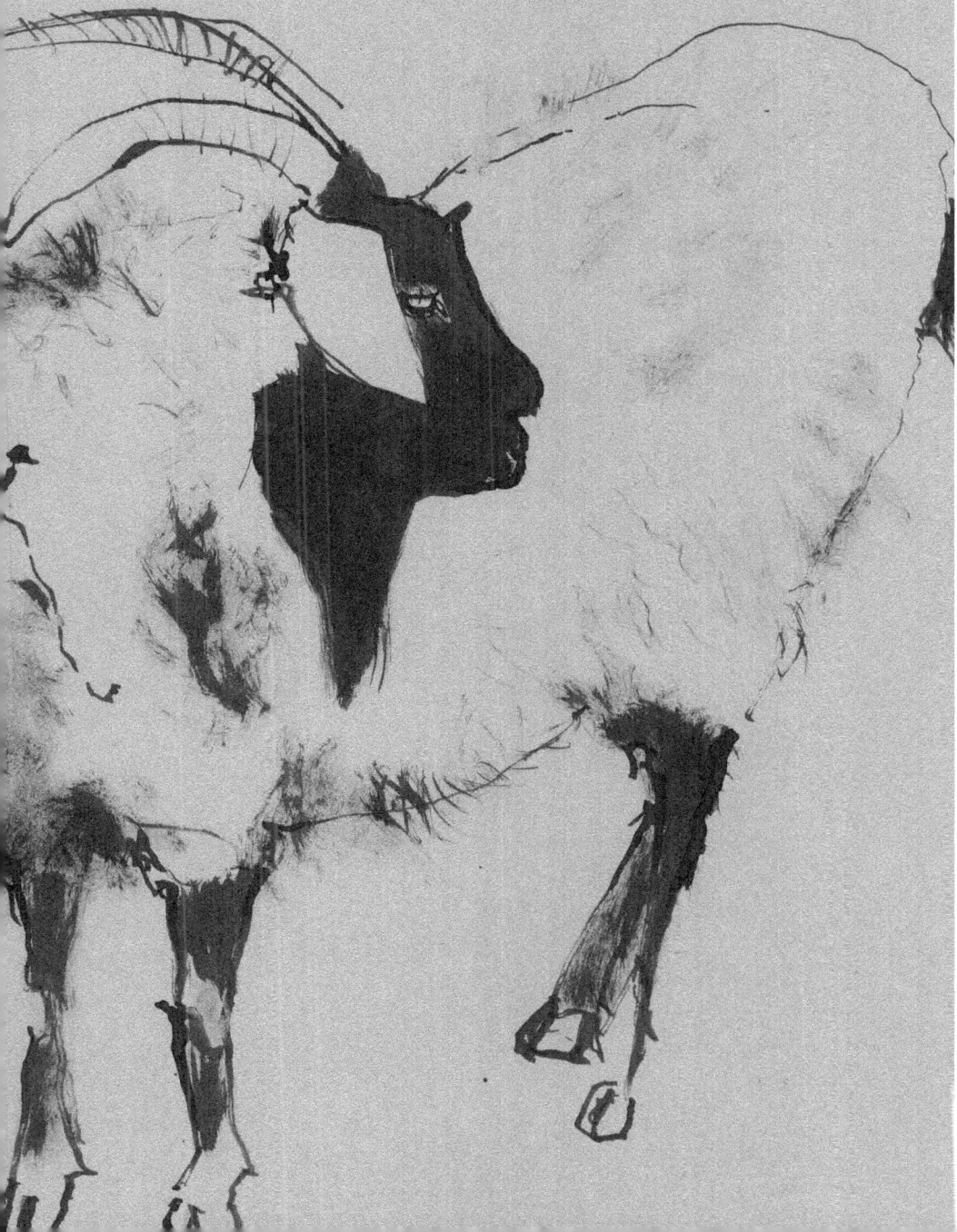

The Paul Revere Girls

Gelignite seamstress I address
You as . .   California

O modern lump of elk, American phur seal check
Dead skunk check   becoming dead skunk check
Whaler's pussy shade and a various shanty I wreck myself on obsessional
    currents that are you

                        Licked mythologies that gt burred on the fault
There is no going back in the way
                    You fancy

In paso de Robles
They're building a town called Paso de Robles its raining
  That black pea-coat you left at Los Alamos
                        Was your home   idiot
                            Coma spare aparts in the raven lots.
Fat farmed oak with the initials from four wars.

Santa Susanna's Aztecs brought to
    Contemplate the single figure of the Christ
Yr. gun-cuckoo nudity and streak
  You still think and spasm
    Like a bird. So bruised.
With affections and Spanish Calculus, got
  Any apple seeds? We'll make these hillsides pay and pay

Yours in the brambles, Sir.

6

Golden leaflets of shoji

Golden leaflets of shoji
  Bitter the track
  I've had my cup of coward's bouillon
The treachery involved in just meeting another person
blue-jays twit the devils
holding a hand to the iron to see the sun
oxide fuss in the off-centre muscle that's the heart
can i be proud of the earth and its damned cells

soft-tiered ruffles that is my digestion   stunning!
Goat-pack hollows   bearded éclair   what made you want to bit
Exactly your lip
  Pressing a cache of blood just there
Il tremblant a lot,

Only because of friction of the thought of what of
Whatever is squalid in your pants
      The blackbird sees!
Blackbirds squabbling in your pants
I most follow you in the exhalation of Abbottsford dew
 (it does not tremble)

 O great bird of suspicioun
goose the temple bell!
Hanover smokes when my baby is in it.
  Sad with a lisp

Sucks to be the gypsy.

(Admire my sheep)

Admire my sheep's tooth

                        Affixed to m. skull where once I flashed
an Admiral gap   Call me Petula . . . Saint,
the Petulant One
our shepherd still sleeps under the row of aggressive pines
slithering is what you call the movement of the snake

One shot with you and I wake to the infinite lurgy.
 All down the river underwear *für damen und herren* float pegged
 Underwear garments   Made with great concentration so far away in
potent shanghai
I belive with grave tenderness
groomed by the sweet and eccentricly heated

Winds of Deloraine secret epistle
Of Van Diemen's Landt
               Stop by the greedy cottage
A quarteracre of Australian Schwarzwald
w/its rare despicables and spätzles
where the Widow Cobcroft will light
a traveller's pipe.

Caisleán Bhun Raithe
Castle at the Mouth of the River of Ratty

Pishogue

Have you every been to *sigh*

Gentle O'Flahetry's

Where the swich liquors   groom you r mind
                  To homelessnesses best dressed

Limerick is beautiful

Exspecially with the sweat,   the gilded triffids and my wholly bandy-
    legged

Friend who were no underpants these last forty miles   check
    her listening pistil

Check   Us   In   to the Hotel Moribund

  On her credit card her name is aisling (pronounce ash-

ling)

        She trowed up her oysters and champagne

       She still thinks the day is darling

             Pick an instant roost.

            We're only here to roost

          Make a reasonable roost

               With you my cockatiel

&Get you off the hanky, the irish whiskey hankey

& I'm thinking of telling my fearther, singer of 'bastard landlord'

&   The Humour is On Me   Now

               As the photographic black of me mam's

hair

        (she had 'great legs'   I've got me mam's legs)

Bomb lovely Derry on the banks of the Foyle.
 The flags are without breathe
    : the pond
snores

Remember the swineherd, the guardian of your swine
Remember me to Limerick that is lovely in women.

Dingle

Spring blaws in my blimey
There she is moving her barrow
  Keeping her sage in the sun's blarney
My wickedness is love of a kind,
No?

How many thresholds are there for kissing at
Now Show Me the kidney of riddles
  There's buttons want popping

O raffish stones, how dark and excitement is it inside a bird And how
    without
The humour's fallen off that one
Criminal beautitude   i called my caravan *'shoshone'* (it was
'The Early Margaret')
  And helped myself to several   affairs

Irish hoaxmen sing *i have a tiny acorn inside of me*
cute Shay Kavanagh   might yow   get me a cup of tea?

At the king's domain we caught about a dozen
  The'sky's bonnet is full o dastardly
  Fat black swans to eat- or
Put the whole thing in a pie and get it down to the Spoleto wind festival
  The last moribund form of that art.

Magnified piccolo that is at first cranial ghosts of childrens voices play
The tundralove of clouds a firm drizzle

Well, this is what I think and to hell with you.

Cork Butter Exchange Brass and Reed Band

Cork Butter Exchange brass and reed Band had better watch out
 What they have I want, shall be mine, the churn, the velvet
]   chearms
Emerging from the lavoratory as the horned young baccchus

Fcken blazed of the forehead
  Patrone saint of mooching and pooching
Who's initials are inscribed on the much-dented instrument that wakes the
    valley?

Dauphine, watching you get dressed is the height of beau-nasty behaviours.
Refrain, darlink, from this overdoing and overgoing
  Gentlerouge of the biscuit-pincers   gentle rogue
 I wake to the perfect recollection of minge on toast

I'm changing my name to bo'clair or
               Tread Eagerly

'Whey bother me little bo'claires'?   but I am pothered

Sometimes i suspect my amourofauna, the smalle cell-people, the ones who
    share my cigarettes
        Bacteriat Barterium
        Who are supposed to love me but are quietly eating me I am the feast
The sacrifice the beautiful bull bits, teats, torso, the head split in twain
My humour chuckles down the steps
        Of the temple

I want you to love me baby, now that we have burned off the smut so to
Sprach.

As the goat with the fangled horns I donate the art
Of getting at one's own behind.

Sheehan.

misfits

Some of the all great time ladies get ready to go to the races.

One with hat made of a leaf and two poach egg.

Hungover and gunsick i wants to drown in some new weeds. Sweet smelling
with a ready

Erection   though peace and evil

Harpers and trumpeters were we,

Hello again, Pat here,

does anyone have a photo of either the turf depot on Lally Road or of Dinny-
Boy Desmond.??

Hi pat gedda logan here just   jimmys in st mary hospital still alive ger
logan x

hi again pat .... and gang i remember u all u were all gorgeous . . ha.ha . . .
ha.ha..myself and yvon down here in meath he doing well
hes happy in himself

it were summer for that halfhour when we all achieved smoking

you biting and sucking on your lip popped and fingering your history

in my coat made of twnty rabbits   shay timon wanted it

labre park has a saint a hen

the tops o the powerlines im sure are very pretty and Ireland green as   cake.

I am opposed to work.

I will sing you a song called 'straddling the moor

He had the dare of the latitude   food stainswagger

The dirty canal   the light industry

Get that feckin unicorn out f the picture

Soft goes the everything

It almost smells like sex
  It certainly smells welcoming
& the Ballyfermot school production of Waiting for Godot
Will you come mostly up Con Corbet Road theres something im sure to show
    you.

myths of St. Bridget.

My surname from Ireland.

My grandparents. My name.

'neck-lace' or 'victorious' i'll be born in Ballymoney.

My mit smells peculiar of Cassandra O'Connell's pussy.

Check the hoof for the health and other things i knowed.

wreck the measure of the candy-earsed Doolan boys.

short on blague they'll .. trains are ringing out of Richmond Station. Joy-
    speck,

egg-punk, vale, a barrow of bourgeois mysteries, my pa chawed

his teeth off by Forty. This town coud use some streamers.

I am with freckles.

I am nasty.

I am fourteen years old.

I *am* to be the hairy beauty spot of your contemplation.

Harpist Bunratty Castle by Clare Stinkboot.

I spent whae whole summer
  Medievalising the fuck out of every t*ing
  Even the Mystique of Women

& spent nights nude in a Shannon farmhouse
  With a plate of suckling pig prepared in the faeshion
                    Of Peking

Synthetic cloverStraw for m. bed, and the Irish
                Airforce exploring
  The dome of paranoia overhead
    I'm ever or never getting away w'it

Bertie O'Hearn Wolfe Tone come come now
              That prick Van Morrison they all drank raw egg
All sang all played as the harpist at Bunratty Castle for a season

Me myself I'm starving the wages to buy an English Wedgewood
JASPER PALE BLUE BUNRATTY CASTLE TRINKET BOX NIB
Shae's a fookin' cracker
Noone gets the castle but I'll get all the kitsch:

Bunratty Rout

I had wanted it to be a calamitous device
Wanted it to be calamity.
Lough Neagh is connected to the rest of Europe by about a million eels.
The name means the lake of the horse-god Eochu

> Lord of the Underworld
> Natürlich

.

None of this matters I'm on a Bunrattie Binge!
A natural putridity by which we like to live.
Devotio moderna　　*Damnatio memoriae*

Cashleen Bun Raith
monument to the detournement of the River Ratty
The castle on the bend of the river of rats

> Soóft have I been honeyskunked and kneaded

licked

> By your careful liquers

Le grand immeublement, being real and unmoveable

> I think I'll watch the rest of the western derby from

here
Hold my hand daerlinks
The labyrinth is terrifyingly simple by design
Culting and occulting it is invariably unicursal

!

I love

Coca-Cola   That industrial-blood colour so sticky on the insides is the
    promise of a whole culture w 'its

 ghostly tremendums

speakin tro'our pipes you'll find this is a dramatization of tinkerdom.

        Begone bygone days of Ireland

  Welcome nitrous oxide consortium of a new pikeydom

'Stabbing the fly with me gypsy fork'   Now what at all was that slang for⸍

E have the last snake of Ireland on a spit

 E have the last snake of Ireland which is me fairly spitting

This Poem is Dedicated to or About That Tempany Bastard Luke Doolan A Jockey.

Today the lambies taste like this
    Tomorrow it will be something other   (deus vult)

The jockey is employed
  Will always be employed
He has soft hands and he smokes
Borrows   superstitions. *Doo'ne speak of those who spail out of the saddle*
Doo'ne let the porte'rsbroome touch ye on the louth.

American-Australian Atlantic clam
Misty   Sam Moginie calls him 'precisely Irish'

He's the inheritor of cowboy slits though no one sees them
Theres mostly a touch of Spokane weevil

'He's really a very small part of it'
Sais the Horse's biographer
'He brands himself with the iron you hand him'

Eclaircissement- lightning explanation of something hitherto inexplicable
He sits the horse like a sparra' but a sparra what's seen a lot of Horse
Flicks
The mouldering air will not contume him.

His fancy plait poked out all weekend, He could rake and ride a twister, throw
    a rope
Charm a toecorn. .confirm the fickle and worming
blood is all of a piece

He corrects lightly and longingly he lets the horse her have head.

Heardly heard   the cock-joint commotion coming from over near Berowra heavily

It is the thunderbird

The grasses conceive these dizzy nitrogen signatures

    It changes the track

For fame and near his sometime wife

Whose name could rhyme with Countess Feebles

   Manipulates her lissome wrists

   Around a recent lover

& eats lightly.

He supplicates with Friar Berrigan, confesses to collecting Marlboro butts

  Marked at their ends with lipstick twitches

Horse bites Hore lips

, horse- crush, horse-temper

Met me in the Calvary clover

This is tyrannous.

He would rather withhold information than give it if that information gave

    the im-

pression of him being any-

thing other than just

like everybody else.   'cepting

one time when he meant to say

'I'm like half the characters in Wuthering Heights!'

Victorian flies are erstwhile citizens of the

World
& scrupulously tidy

w/ their scruples

Cuadrilla.   (Ignacio Sanchez Mejias)

To die beautifully and gangrenously
   In a two day ambulance trip through rampant Spain
By turns you love Bernadette Soubirou and Marcelle Auclair

The suspension is crystal with ice and oranges in slices
Who can think of biography when out the window the black branches replay
    like favourite
Lorcaescas   (hello Fred, chubbie and gorgeous with ciggie-in-hand
The Andalusian sun does make dark plates of your mooch and your eyes
   Matadors shadow coaxes the mythos of the mouse

An over-the-hill bullfighter   sunk and tranquil
He had no car, no hotel, not even a *cuadrilla*
Pinky ring, dust from the boiler, black Seville suit, balance yourself one dizzy
       vines on the side of the Warm house,
the gravel sounds, the carriage returns, inside the horsepower is the centre of
    the
earth
:iron

Cordoba, and what is not composed of Raven bop
 A plait of silk placed at the throat   and will smell like you forever   till o
    pansies turn to
rotten
:sugar
   The mole which hangs in the orchard above your lip and below your careful
     part
  Imported harpies in greeting cards asphyx and disappear
  See the whipsed white lines on our trouser?

Weve been walking in your Salt

  We roll by all the paintings of the   reconquista
Only to remember the blacks and yellows of the shagging wasps

Garlic bob on a saddle-pommel
thrye taking my wife in the other direction

Clever nip of the first ants in my stockings I can see the Dutch attraction to
    still life
O bully bull i don't blame you or your super-taper
Horn
What is more possibly intimate than murder

What Would You do Without Me? Explorer's Lament. (Note found with the remains Of Humidore Wyatt.)

I woke up in Spittal and
    I don't know how but
the morning moon is in the South and
       it never is. Odd. And
Ugh.

Not hungover I count the skulls inthr. container
       Rolling like Pepperkorns

I have a tiny botanist's aspiration
       Close to your buds
The smell of you on your left side of me
    Is pure propaganda.
Why don't we jig anymore instead of lugging
Blue potato bags is't a
    Vast calumny?

O don't starve yourself cottonlegs.
Winter breeds in the backs of trees   knit knit
  Winter composes hues, doesn't it?
       Hues and soups.
Note how there's no
     Slang for piano   like
'busterguts' or 'black mmoby dick' or 'Consuela's martyr'

I love this winter he's
After saying it maketh Time
    Consumptive.

I am in my tent.
  I ate my huskies
  but not the fur.
One last read of
  'cigar aficionado'
    magazine
 then to
    Expire.

The Duke of Maggots

In a dream Duke Maggotski saying 'I am   Nobody'
Wháppears as Charlie Manson wháppears as Gram Parsons
          Shuffle shuffle
Faith has been broken   Tears must be cried
Bunny Rogers   Eileen Myles
 Sedeuced.

What is it that is moving in your blood do you know are you required to
          know?
Simple breakfast of hog and grains
          A walk to the ice-parlours of Mentone
I feel I have split my honky-tonk bladder so this
          seance of   shitty superfluity

You find 'ts a story I'm telling 'ts not for you but your centenary

                    aggots

Or the tiresome brain whae socializes w'itself over a serfdom of blood
          sausage
 Pushy!
          Evidently tripe has overrarching ambitions of freedom..
Thádmirable Celtic league of defeatists.

Chan Marshall marries me again with the ballad of Willie Dead Wilder and
          Rebecca
          I wake with my legs in the air as the salute to bachelor squalor (hey
          mamma!)
A sweet gyppin' like a long sodden
 I came for the Viking horror and stayed for the chanter
   Though I note yow have chucked my flow'ry tribute in the river

O, Not so fast frills, not so fast

      S'Long as we're still 10% furry   and battye!

              i   n   t   e   r   m   i   s   s   i   o   n

Could we be having a little more spook from the pipes thair Mairtin?

      Fairn, boyo

          r   e   s   u   m   e

      Only you, sweet culprit

The perfect shade of what you have seen lies with you

      Encased as a nipple of garlic, too sensitive in its exquisite hues

Side A I got a girl call'd Boney Maroney Side B You Bug Me Baby.

Anyway last night was worth it so I could casually use the word 'histrionics.'

Th'humans as they appear put phantoms to shame fortunately

 We only do love the phantomns.

Give me More Golden Tantrums of the West.

Il Gattopardo

Theleopard picked up daddy & kissed him under his forechops
 Bending with The sumptuous candles

 I haven't lost an eye I wear my badinage as a charm, a sort of scapegrace,
    and anyway
Don Fabrizio, Bert, is a long time in the bath

Generous of the toilet, for his cologne he is dependent on Sicily, he is as gay
As the bullfighter's croquette, though fatherly, masterful, and before
    democracy
Squeamish

The last aristocrat of this sort of thing was also the first
Monday and I'm wearing the black ribbon I found on yr daughter's floor
Musn't one have a favour to tie on one's grip?

'Marlboro' means a little flirting with death at the milk-bar puffpuff
The weather today a dirty martini

G.Herders still mauve their goats up the side of the volcano)(sicilysicily)
Dressed not by the fur and wool eye of Visconti but

Th'heavenly Deirdre of a cocktail hangover
Hearing of revolution, the Don goes to his fleshpots.
In the figure of the flicker, how does the woodpecker
                Fit so dearly?   Is it his flexion

Garibaldi, his beard, his Napoli bonhomie
'hah! I want to bring him alive so I can Kill him again!'   (say what ..)

One suspects a sexy spectre   illogic of the martyr
He will never be dead enough

O no, no, it's you we love Il Leopardi
& the crack ducks of Sicily.

Peckvillon.

Dear D'Arcie Davey, Im writing you From the dead heart of Carolton
You mangle m'imagination with your downtown \curtsey

   (courtesey)

  T'occurs as a kind of gorgeous pugilism

      Just exciting enough without being overwhelming

Fatal winds at a fatal cross-roads (now *stop* it!)

      I think I finally got my satisfaction as in a duel I feel

It has taken half my life to lose the shame of being a thief.

      Call me *Peckvillon*

      Blessed peace of the sated predator.

Born of the bourgeoisie one becomes a poet to partake

      C' peasant (o my teeth, daddy!) and Aristocrat

so simple:

 Nankeen embroidered jacket, white Marseille vest buttoned

               'a vary little way up' fine linen shirt with the collar

               'thrown over in such a way as to almost uncover his neck'

Short buff laced boots sometimes worn with garters

   & a pile of decayed Cheshire cheese, w

                           An immaculate and dainty turbot

& a casual selection of pickle

Partage of the nipple truffle, the plucked ambergris
black charged handsome not noble or shy far from it

      with a white lick o'th' terror (& a hiho Silver)

         air creamed of sarsaparilla double-dealt with the heart

& its slurping entendres

When love's Infection is Live it is a singeing
      Thing
Pikies   Minks   Gadgies & Tinks
  What we love is a smattering of factions.

A tattler, a prot, a jailybird

      Je m'appelle *Peckvillon*
       Blessed peace of the sated predator.

I lay on the train embankenment and have the engine trim the air about
                           Because I am a bon vivant a black
  Melancholique as though some semi-divinity
Has thought 'In this one I love craven-ness and in that the cock-sure spree, but
  in you,
        Cherie, we shall love
               Our morbid capacity

The friendliest of Titans, you recall, got a lot of trouble
         Retrieving for us   unbidden
le feu

Bad Luck Continues for Captain Cleland 1870.

The donkey's name was Mistletoe.
Mistletoe. What a bitch.

very impressive , this song, how it is sung, the daring whistle ..   a perfect
    disgrace
ghosts of the armpits I haénjoyed clingen to the mind like abalone so like
                                                                    abalone
one in particular I oft declarred 'ma favourite part of Australia'

located as it was (is) upon the sweetest fuck in the Western World (thóle wirld)
    (vraiment)
 godbye shiralee

other ghosts of military chapeaus seem to hover in the poem, in description
what elas can they do, stupid chapeaus .. hover, hover

Some melancholy german opera sharpens the shadows of the pines At Cowes
  Saying 'Bad luck Captain Cleland, precious tatterdemalion'
The gypsies in the kitchen is softslang for   CRABS

'That, Sir, was an innings of unremitting banditry.'
I have had as I said a certain debauched seizure but soft
 Like tow young women playing knucklebones
His Snakeskin boot still retains the Eye of the serpent that is most marvellous
 The gaze of the marplot, the arch-interpreter, the jealous snot
    Whose name portains the plotted cylinder of light.

 There shall be consturpation.

New England Clam Chowder

Sea Chanteys

Somehow preluding was all the scene
On the English ship pussie-hall
    H.Melville.

Far days on the mizzen-mast

                    deshabby as the scarecrow

  I;m pleased with my employment, I rejoice

I think of my honey-pussy, i think of the stray pony

           I had meant to pur-chase of something serious

Avast,

                   the lavish scroff that quiets the lips

In the pre-cordial mist, all ir harpoons are bent and canny,

             Ranked to buggery, Off the Azores

The harpoon has the job of attaching the whale to the boat and exhausting
    the whale.

To cure estrangement, bite through the wrapper

  There is no centre to the sea it's all an uncommon bog, 'hearties'

    Rare stinks and polyps, natural to shipping thought

O spermy, whae turns sea to fat, I turn fat to song, sea into

  Polyps

'dont look boys; I'll look for ye'

And in such and such a place as

This

  I might make mention of the Milky Way. I Might

And I might not

I folly kiss you on the neck, I mean aplace my lips aparted

Because you are Libya, are you?

Yes. You are salt,   my streak o'lean   insister of fish bones   black stellar

    dessert

 my ships-biscuit my layered chow my cup

                        Of heavy cream my vault

    Of spermacetti

my chaunting

    & fluked

Moby Dyke.

Lamb Chantey

Woodpies lurk near what may be a very fancy shantie
 Wild clover up close is the detail of compromise
 Hey noddy noddy
2 loins form a very grand roasting joint known as the saddle

Soft bickering of your teats I prefer
Your preference of weeding in the "nude"
The choler deepens to a purplish red in mutton

Hey lolly lolly
Historically two-tooth was very important, especially to country families
The fousand tiny hairs out the nose out the ears are bowled and chirmed by
    the wind
Hello middle-age, hello bone-flutes and summer's corpses that go pop

How do you pronounce Eurydice? Why is caring for a rifle and loding
                              It so sexy
One attends to one's musts or lets the will go to   vapour
The promise of alcohol and the promise of song orders the blood about

Obediently like a flock of well-loved lambies: there it goes to the foot
    There pesters the gut, carrying off sausage, there it festoons
The cock to take charge to tink tings over, to speak gladly and finally
              To rest
Thismorning I cleaned my teeth with stew I think I want to
              Smirch and be smirched

Lobster Chantey.

"fair fucks an' you're shittin me to Trixie"
 Song of the contestant to the rose of Tralee

I had 'Shirley' wrote on my boob
    I knowthing about Shirley but
I had wanted to be Banshee

Note wheydontcha the hour
    Of my tremendous modestie

Twas all for plea-sure: now I'm dingling from Tyburn's Block
The doughty price of one's libertine
Age
    Persewed maladvisedly
Tyke hearties my pretties, though I've been a disappointment
 From the scaffold the view is greater, of Schroon bay/pond
  The rumptious cuntling of the sea, the Tipperary shivers
                    Of   firtree

Make me a final meal of Lobster bun and curls of butter
Made by hand three month ago
 In poor old burnt Dunalley.

Pembroke Chantey

Unidentified girls of Pembroke sing
The sea was so rough and my hands is so tough
  A long time agoooo
Blow-boy-blow- - my diggyman
Drunkdrunkdrinky
  It goes on like this actually goes on like this coming out of the walls
            In a vicious glandular whisper

Did the stones learn it from the girls aurora borealis
Songs of the girls trapped in stone ,
wind in the chimney fattens then rakes the fire
Pentecostal polish on my collar
Mixing in the sheen flakes of death

Fly ont' the spit of strathspey re-born again to die on whale-jaw hill
The stench of the white man precedes me

 Here come Pegasus, bags loaded, walking sideways, it is not only our fancy.
Hi Peggy, on this rottenest of days the sun comes out to appal.
Black Polly Harvey's out of breath, deliberately stumbles in her plucking
 The most beautiful, the most insouciant, still craven
Polly
            . .hurtling
            Then wandering the chalk groves   hand in the hand

Louche, douche, I perve on you in the showering can
 The air still burnt with our conversion.

Morning with Ernest Louis Matthewsand breakfast by boat-

Frying eggs on a flint of tin, watch the birds of extinction

Caper

Look away from the earth, where the atmosphere and its inert lover
    twitches, the commingling licks
exchange of cumulus rump, voluptule
fire among the bitches

As we cusp you remarke on that pleasnought smell
Some sort of . . . sea-keg   rides the continuous albas   above
    yonder

Make your head as rough as possible
        A major dirge oafs the lung
As we make way with square oars to the Blaskets

Charm of a bivalve chantey

sharpley and with hardly withouten effort I prise from you
a sigh, not the vaste soupir (oh.) of the sea
    something more morbidly flushed
p.haps a 'radiant travesty'

                    au revoir, Club-toe!

I am airs cheerful as I ought to be   [GODDAMMIT]
    & you can tell by the jauble
        that this is sung
        in le langue gelée
                  spoken in jelly
      "it should have 'spitoon' in it"

What is a bivalve?   What is behavior?

not sphinx but spinx   don't gender the enigma
    Dear Bridie McCarrotty
    Sister to Mellamurphy
He's got a song to sing but it's not about you

Dear Sir   I am fallen in love with a pipe. Your pipe.
  Item: Smooth tadpole tobacciana pipe, grit to suck
  surface issues and teeth chatter
    ouch and very fine!

<<See the restitution of angelic bisexuality>>

joined in enflamed opposition
    round like a colloquoy of major and minor demon tongues
cured in raw bivalvoline.

I once methought we should have our bones thrown in together
Now I'd be pleased if our singing and kissing-bits
 Beput in the one can of langues en gelée

Hand Cramp Shantey.

I would make jewels of your sparkplugs baby   *wait*
I have made jewels of your sparkplugs baby
Orgasms they can be tiny like the sudden elevation of
                                        type or
The word 'muddledly' makes me mind
            The surcharged violence of my days
                        Finagling and fingering our softest bonds

                        The intimate insect history of Melbournen known to me
        now
                                                        Known to
        you
It is tres tres charmant.
I will always love you though
I am not there to love you

The Springe Squalles which batter (bartleby) the house
                Are only vaguely Satanic but fresh!
Fresh my bitterns, my little holly seeds my private ejaculate
                        Cramps
and calm so calm with a calm which even though intermittent is better than
        nothing (Lucky)

Edmund Spenser, that frillsome scourge (of Faeyre Queen Qualification)
    Is burning still in clover hell   Is there an Irish hell
You only knownen there is
Club Pagan where I s'often make my repast

There In Piss Meadow I find a little flattery

                                Of raven Quills and one can't help th emotes and

    mites

That get in you and up you like seed and turbodiesel

    Smogge

with a click of the throat well make a song to modify your brisket.

What is smarter or more lovely :

The English sharpen their attack with Scottish self-loathing.

It is always to be like this- the whole spectacular world gouged out by a

    disappearing

                                    floxie

so far from confetti and the races

Pea and Cream Shantey

You cook the peas in the cream,
                    Ever sae light-ly, bosun, ever sae light-ly

            Who said it was boring getting in boats and chasing the whale
                The dareness of it,
                            The pounds, pounds of spermaceti, liquid Eros in
        that dark

                                                                    &

        Rushing
    Love-tank
                    Plucking roses or pruning the bejingles
                                                    Of your-
        missus, your cutey poops
    Th'harpoon sae sharp I tell you it aches
                    To feel of something, some positive report of disappearance
                        The thin thin flag gales away at the
        toppermost
            purple chortle of garlic, kept in the pockets as a chearm
                        As hard for rage as a heart
                                        Size clutch of aged speck is
        soft to the tonsure

All fish are peace loving even the dicky-shark it is we
                                Who give hem the joint to be 'hell-bent'
                As a carnivore eats a carnivore the gods don't sulk
                                The y may spit into the carpet like
        one paid in beer and tartan

What cry, what aliemental gallop will get us the mark?

Sure there's groats enough inside ye, and snail, cochlea, sea-biscuit,

hammies

All these will make the slaughter,

All the while a-singeing

'Simply going for

Chowder'

I haveso in my gullet a tender jaunt of sea-bug

Imperfect coked

For mine is the chaunters employ, I mauve my tongue in

the topgallant

Faccion

To bring it all about,

Boys

Ive got ambergris behind the ears and Earl

Rochester's strong taste for sea-cadets

Jibs &

Quivers

How can he know what it is to lobster if he's never tried being

Th'buttered lobstee?

Horse Meat Shantie

(beginning with a line of Saxon Prose of my own devicing)

Hir and thir the floccus of clood and the floccus of floom

Agony grazes with a suddenness   that is not at all sudden

Like the Satanic buzz of a horse meat chantey

cool flanks of a Marino marini

Horse with a perfect ass-hole\

The drama is in the texture of the hide- a drop of spit on the coif of the spur

simplify your life, tighten on the flanks

regard!

th'absence of lustre that is the horse:

we dine full solemnly   with a radical piety

our prad is becalmed: our horse knocked up

Where modesty would have me look away well I won't

Bend with the flavour my little sea-beard; your thinking on this is exquisite

is it

It is anyting like waltzing with Cindy Borman

(slowburn Cindy) (swoon)

It is good to drinke in a morning to charmen the mist.

Doodle da de doody etc.

I cannot remove my fat

cigaerette for your kiss Miss Borman, señorita, we must love

around it.

You would be my maculum. A dark spot. A permanent one.

Drunkards on both sides Drunkards

46

What I love about the bagpipes it has the gossip of the cosmos
                                                    Behind it

                    this rancid prescription from Doctor Destouches
                    stringy cavalier
a motley mince of horse and bald rider
those brains themselves when mixed make the most foical
                        matter
aswerve from the bone it is   too too toothsome

Th'day is flush with biomorphs, little corbies becoming
little abbotts
Ill have the seigneur's initials burned on my bittocks
A ploughboy then a playboy

There is no horse-meat chantey.

Can of Spam Chantey.

I will arouse and go now, and go to Innisfree whr.
  The Devils Love Mountain Dew

Your speach, my lttle crozier, cumquat, croquette
                    may lack   spittle
God and Satan both air the most eloquent in Hebrew

Alone Discoursing the virtues of drunkenness and poachingness
 Alone with the Hungarian solace of the stinging gizzard
Va fangoulo baby, it's unpleasant but necessary

You are attracted to the things of stupifiddity because of their names: Bob
    Minty surfboards,
(Bellbrae   Bellambi   Broulee)
        The hanging gibbet at Portree, Laprohaig, Bruichladdich, Inverrarity
   Single flame single curse vapours   whisper your name mincingly
   An almost debauched degree of barley   a connoisseur's vocabulary
                              To thicken then thin the blather
I have a head for Saturn
I, a talking magpjie, salute you my master with a distinct voice
 Unrolling the cans of spam shantey

If you have a passport you are sort of welcome at the cannibal's feast
 Unbeknownst to themselves the maggots have finished the fare and now eat
    of each other

I read at night in Lornenen and go south in the winter
 To sit on the porch and whistle w/ ma madrigalised mama

In Bonney Van Diemen's Landt

A tragedian without a tragedy.

Crack- Rabbit Shantey

Smack-kissed and munificent
I'm frying testy devils on the tops of my kidneys
  I went to bed with details of the rabbit poacher's
                              Racket &
Awoke to the clobber of Duncan B. Bonaparte.

O fourth and quietest horseman
    Of the Western Derby
Do I have time for a piss and a fiddle?
  Or must I sing my part in this Apocalyptic kitsch

        Doing the Charleston in a firestorm.
Systematistemicisms of over-regarded and gorgeous tripe
  It's aliementary   One cannot find the end or the beginning
                        Pick pick
If 'things themselves' are very cheeky it's because they been taking dexies
Breakfast for example looks like a Chaim Soutine today
            Seasoned with Landlord's Grippe

It comes on sanely like a pack of goats with glorioles
        Not nimbus haloes or aureoles
          Th, nub of the horn is visible from certain angels
        Then one knows who one has been dealt
            Ooh là là

O don't I really desire a domicile of mine own
Make me then a mosaic of a cross-eyed Apollo.
The spirit world is this world 'taint no difference that a number of the dead

Are as unlovely as some of the living

Now how could I be putting words into that pretty little mouth?
There is always some Club Buggery about it O well
Heraclitus says
  Laughter is a killing thing.

Drag Racing Shantey

Ilove to listen to yr crackling baby\
  The plastic glamour of the animal for ages

Sausy little bitch that I yam
          That I yam
 Sausy little bitch that I yam
  (well he isn't)
Is there a shantey to time us as we
      Shampoo the mole
         Bunratty
           Bunratty
What have you in your go-betweens t'sustain you
                  T'sustain you
What have you in your go-betweens that will never but let you down.

Landscape is only achieved because certain things have been razed
                           Removed

  they yet

                          Remain
To haunt the living jigger in us.
Afollow a trail of thumblets of black whiskey
                  Stupeforte
W'Her French (strong) tail in my mind I winder
  The foalds of the hills of Broago   M. shadow which I follow
        Holds a mess and measure of spook.

Encloased bounty come to me be mine.
The burning red foax, the guilty Tipperarys

I poach a pair of gifted feathers   Felice

Rovers knew the pranks of proproiety
  The reappearing fence (there's only one fence-

    Continuously)
With a chirrous liver and a growth of petrol dollars at the hip I'll go a
    Roving
Headers Stackers Wadders   Crackers
  Be still my darling its only a Drag Racing Shantey

Snottische.

Richmond hotties are hotter than other kinds of hotties but harder
\   to find (trobar trouver)
They may not even be hot at all
There is a man with a bag of tripe.
I wonder is he thinking 'Tripe Shantey?'

The hands give it away a little bit
The hands give it away every time
The hands give away nothing   (prokoffief   sneaky
    bitch!

Last night I was t the pub with five people I wanted to fuck at some
                                       Time &
Last night I wanted to fuck them all last night!   Hiho &
Aukenward.

Gorgeois Karen (Black)   we called her 'Death Bags Murphy'
Death bags Nasty. Death bags goes to Hollywood
\   as shae did
Which is this poem except that the real we
Sit in Richmond over late lunch for breakfast (for which we fight the supper-
    fly)
Judge the faccions of others with a less than sporting eye
Laugh rippishly – you know – 'the flickering little victory'
O my bonton bébé be my little
Cobra in a box?
Xx

Vida: Nora Pike was married to a Victorian Lord, and spent much time at court in 'Melbournen' <which means at once 'everywhere a swamp' and 'Triggertown'> Though she references others in her songs she seems to have been the only trobairitz of this place, and so she seems to have believed whatever pleased her. She made and sang many fine *sirventes* and *canso*, was red in the fur and was oftent' called 'the greatest of gingers.'

Poem called laphroaig (Dedicated.)

His wedding boot was rupled
 His pecker is set straight (like Wyatt)
Let us speck of knightage: knights collectively

Let us specke of the expansion but not the breach\
Like when a king eats a king I'll have the bones for my garden
Please   &
Fisticuffs.
I want to fickle you in our summery affliction of too much summer
His soul and his wife's are actually like a sheet of gold leaf
                   Or corned Beef.

It is not necessary to Live and Think
  But to bloat to the point of peccability
pêle-mêle plural pêle-mêle
th'affectionate tickling of painful grapes

m'aime comme l'idol formé de la form redoublée et derangement
m'aime

Eilean Beag (small island)

Celtic stockings made from beard of the fetid goat
  Gingerre, marmalady, Loblolly: all products of the Western sun
beChristy!
      & I have fought the admiration
Of some terrible bogeys.

Imported fetisches of every kind
Chur chur
  The double spined blacksnake ... golden logie of the th'antogoniste, th
    importunate one
A psychological farm that manages the intersection of placable names
  Chevalier D'Entrecasteux   Lalah Rook   Truggernana
    Bucky Maynard
                  G.A 'tidy bitch' Robinson
                  G'vrnr Arthur

Mum smokes Lady's Preferentials and Pall Malls
Dad smokes Walter Raleighs
      (Well matched they could spit equidistantly)
   & we prise into the cocky's joy

Old Prick of Sea-iron, I suck my gravey sauce at the Hero of Waterloo &
    think

                        On Trefoil Island

La plus aggressif

                  Island of them all

                  Can you feel the whole mass shaking?
Generous mouthfuls of gorgeoius white blubber
   It's the slide toward dandification I'm afraid

Unlimited pricks garlanded (attended) w/ pricklets!
O Where have you been charming
      Billy Boy Bailey?

Ir bogus vision has excluded the Heavy Devils
'fuck' has been lovingly repossessed for the commons
 'fornication' keeps its serpurnt purchase on the flesh

                             meine pussy-willow

The body as elaborating gibb'rish machine, unholy support for the tongue only
 Like any whistler's favourite it ends its apocalypse at the beginning

Criterion Hotel Gundagai.

They wore garlands of wild Parsley
Sappho

Woodpeckered.

I don't know that I've been told, something 'bout your jelly-roll

They have proverbs in Hell Shane Dooley I wonder if they are memorable.

After all William Blake went down the river with Nobody.

Well take this in begorgingly

Will the villain be soon in our storey, Sirrah?   I do like a Villain.

They keep up the sordition and they pretend

To keep us seducted.

I hear Werner Herzog narrating us already, so that we see ourselves for the
idioten we are

The racing scapegoat   *c'est moi.*

@ The Criterion Hotel Gundagai

The maître de chef knows only one word   Diabolo   Diabolo

His name is Gesualdo.

There is a golden firebird in the valley   the size of a child's fit

It behaves with utter coquetry   by never being seen

Gundagai has a real 'village' feel to it   *tu crois?*

A boxer   A spastic   A mauruader   Maugre Triponions

A Queen

The trees around dance on the hills like little black devils in the plural
  Demoneii
Rusted railway nodes lay about as littered cursives, the sinking punctuation of
  an Imperial
jig

                    Stupefacted
Ribald hip-position
            The lost verses of a Gandy Dancer

I do know that there are often quiet third- party
            liquorice shade-spots on the southside Southern Murrumbidgee

I cured myself this morning with a sausage of some antiquity
            Maintaining a view or your crystal knickers
I paint black clover, in the mud flats cruel with black clover   I call
    it
Horse_Running_Without_Jockey
            The Nervedness of it

I've over a dozen donkey hides on the keep but I think I'll go nude
            Though this is not to be free

Naughty o'hearn gavest me

The blackest dollar I ever saw

& just in time my set of sulphur fetishes   breaketh and bleaketh
    on the humid wind

O principle minx, who holds my mit in the curlewed thighs, bush-stoned
    curlywed thighs
 Your many ornaments, which are madding of shells, of violet parrot feather
                Now archived now in a very private hell

godbye favouritted narcotic
 the garbage boy is fo'lorn

attend me <attendez-moi!> my boastful sea-flunkys, the girl I lovede is
    gone
 Gone with the gift of the sacred sheep, shae whom with we made a
    romanticated

               Abalone shantey
'tis croked
 In the tall town of Hobart I take refuge in the Saxon keep, w/its three
    wolves and a clutch of
Barley
The oracle states: if you proceed, you will by that gentle hand
       be flam'd like the bombalaska!
    Yield!

I thank of the titles of our adventures: Pure furr   Walhalla   Hare
    March Ballarat

&

The fickling suite of the Shamrock Hotel

Once there were these little forays all over France (I want you to stamp my
ass with your

lobster!)

O my little Nemesis, my fruiting muff

Or are you Nyx?

Goodbye your tantalitic lisp, your not so straight foxteeth

You altogether are toothy

nightshade,

Who steps thro- the crack in the gate foundled in a leopard shimmer
Rather than labour with the latch and are gone

Drambuie

an dram buidheech

Noone knows I live and have lived in Peckerville Street / Horny horny
    blackbrd
What is convivial in spring's early sprocket
Th'poor download pictures of porkchop
For the slavering over
It is the season of fresh waltzes
            & clysters
Bungleboys
I count the little salt christalhs on th Jam of Serrano ham
    My lady procured for moi (up the sleeve) (send the po*lice*!)
There'splenty buttons want popping in a XXAGGERATED FAESHION
    (Hello

    Bufftone!)
Such Nobilety
  Are they porcine tears one should forward to the poor?
                    To spice there gruel? (yes, my gentlephogies)
I've had my 'twae baked beans a la gourmand bitch'
    From Mrs Moleys Cookbooke for the Shitting poor'

  Time an go for a Blazey!

I've a com:pressed nerve in the Bacchicals
            Just exciting enough w/out being Overwhelming

Tekkin' my Beardrouge for a walk T'meet
                    T'other Beardrouges   aravin
    W/ supersticciouns

And the light seems to be eternally gruby and the joy
    Requires this simple partage

Impudicizia Ricchezza.

It's Bailey or Bust!   Nick Whittock

As the myour of Merimbula I am banned from Pambula bot
I shall return as the Wrighteous Gorgon of Mimbula and Perambula

Dirty Roxy driftout from Twofold Bay in the SS Corky Corkson
    Whae' thrives on steam, gammarays, oil of pneumonia and the laement
            Of all the dead Marlin, plucked for sport from the sexy
    waters themselves

Rich in impudence I invented certain phantoms   Whom I gave the soft
    joins of humans
Now I jump like a bliggard whenever they call
        *** & am tres desole when they don't or willn't
Take me home to **Pole O'Shea** with her fickle brassiere whose catch
                I cannot discover
Her deadfleck rouge and lipstick cartridges made with and paid for by
    whaling
Count me as a stinkspot in your cosmic seismographologue   caught in the
    loop of Scorpio's tale
I have only my chapeau Napoleonique fattened like Byron's
        & a bit of sea rope to hoist my trouser
            The length of my faith

    I haeve the strangest power of speech.

Preacher's Blues

M upholstered skull is a place of exalted gloom, each skull is a temple

A rodential temple

Th'time for venerating the protoplast (the fuckn what?)

Is gone

Gone with our subcaudal supserstitions

Evie's mishap

forgotten

I think I'll stay at home and finish 'The Banshees of Inisheer' as a favour to
Morteen

McDonaugh

Following senile Sophocles therre'll be three characters who all have dined too
oft'

At the Golden

Hypocrite Hotel

Ismene, Antigone and

Gig Ryan

They're none of them hypocrites at all at all.

Sold a belt by a pikie, loaded with supernumerary charms, to keep up my
preacher's pants

In th'blissfulle morn I see it is a child's belt

Narcissus became the God

of our world.

On S'occupe

I pace the floor in m little satin devil-boots.

Behind Broulee

A sweet left breaks in front of
 Bombo train S_n.
OHara gits a Red Bonnet
 Slipper-de-bits comes in at Bendigo-on-the Radio

Silked by Black Clover cubed.
Imlay wants me now 'm Mayer
                    Of Merimbula, I think of Elvis his liver..

                                                    Caca.

Pair of framed red panties framed inside
 Milton tyre service
 Mechanical! Repairs (*Ullafuckingdulla!*)

 & Rd. Whskrs on ma
                Mayoral robes (doughty bastards of scupperance) o well
O new helmets designed for a more sensual experience on the pitch!
So that we might become or be
                'More complete beasts'

The Maban to sing you must first get inside you though you know this
        already
 Betestacled and filliant I wanted to be Brigadier but wake to find I have
        come
 To be the Bastard of Broulee.
Dick Turpin III
        The Bonny Prince's face
            Wants smashing in

beBlightey!

Coney Island

I've been to many paradies.
In the blister-haze at Loch Neagh we charm it ourselves by being there
Tickled in turn by the Crumlin, the Glenlavy, Moyola, Ballinderry
  We cut yr cake on th 'original Coney Island   (*Innisclabhall*   bitches)

The fox crossed the frozen lake and got all 26 hens. (lttle drool there)
On and on over the hill and the craic was good

The hot mizzle, the feather mess which is mine, the wattle-shot which is yours
  Beer, when good, 'tis called 'the creature'
Sticks o'Ham candy
  Proletariat ecstasies   the class system is a bugger
                          I hear in a bluessong by Hairlip Dupree
    passing by

Great big chunks of Atomosphere   The world's uterus
    explodes

                  I wish
        I was picking you up in a Cheverolet Caprice   hot air outside
  yr mama's birthday
      hotter inside as the engine chuckles & contemns
              Great big Chunks of atomosphere.

Title: The Dauphine Goes to Town
Title: The Dauphine distributes her footstink
Title: The Dauphine consults the hoi-poloi for her notions

Send me some one delectable from your barrages de richesse!

I still love it   what?   Ireland's fucked'dness.
 Where do you leave your boogers now Cheroot
                        I mean Cherie.
I want to take this opportunity to thank Appalachian Heaven   I'll
    never go

My name is Fléance.

Trimballage

Beelzebub my dear, woldn't you start me up a Cant-town Shantey?
<Pipes begin>

I would climb Mount Chamonix (i.e. the smallest hill in Gundagai) with a
  Bowling ball in each hand
For you babycakes   Thank God I dont have to I'd rather
  go

a-Rutting

One makes a scape goat, and keeps it, and feeds it
        This Helps accrue the Satan figure within the creature.
        I would climb Mount Azazel in order to instruct
            All goats shall go free!   O baby Repent!

Where do you tender those turning armpits now, modeste parotte?
Certains. There is a glow along the rotting olives

The coroner's coat lay across the bed in our little room.
I have two postcards here; one from Frank 'Il Leopardi' O'Hara
  Being ….. Liverish
& Tóther from yourself, which puts me to mind of you writhing around
  In your nightie like a naughty albino labrat, another corrupted production
done in

        Lost Doves Press Type

I'm slowly baking a sentimental cult & I want your hand in it
m/pretty.

\

Photographs of Lightning May Be

    Blasphemin' but Feels   Totally

                              Great

Bronwyn Frances, my nsughty exgirlfirnd, is traipsing the paddock

    somewheres traipse

                traipse

A paquet of Nix   A pure opium racket

                   Telegrammed anarchy

          On the sweat buttocky hills of Tallarook

Take me to the Cock O'Lairpin

    Or Carrionblush Hotel I think I'm feeling

A little fancy.

The flaming giblet's guide to amorous vassalage.

Thin lipp'd, physically and metaphysically, yow have ackscended
 From Bohemia to Haughtalage

                              Darling O'Guile.

Whatever it is is looming

                    Plumply   - it shall describe this day fo'rver

I parted (pearted) with a thimbleful of ladypiss on loan to Faerye Meaddow
     clop clop
 Dingling and strangling in a band of advaunced satanistes (let's call it
     dabbling)

                    You are incapable of being mingled

We had a horse call'd Blush she was a Bitch ... at the earliest opportunity
     necking the rider
 On low branch   who could blame her blame her

The skys is full of Royal clouds- Bourbon, Charlemangey, comfortable and
     sinister Drapery
 our sacks full of ruminant pleasantrys
   our gorgeous silence rippled like the pox

the cool refuse of conflagration, ashes whose curl is 'petulance,' the lashes of
     Our Lady

                              warm   calculatrix
Delaying infinitely the work that is to be done our distractions become our
     histories.

What is unforgivable ... ?

　　Etcetery etœtry

We risque a lot on the fumes that reach us 　　from afear 　　　　from

　　Chateau Pesquie

Oedipus Rex

My own crow-roads where I believe accidently kill the father, he being myself
 enwizened with

               A flattened liver
Wz betwixt Cobargo and the Bitchy of Brogo (like a duchy but with amore
 supernal twinkle)
A cockatoo haughtily resigned to auto-death
 King Billy distribbutin his sophistry came this way impeccably dress'd
As does a mauldy replica of Mad Max's XB Coupe
 Elle noisy Windsor smallblock V8   of sauvage chearm

           'mekkin pilgrimage' as Big Bill
 Chaucer would say

 Sick of what may be dappling we decide on crystal fibrillating
      One only gets ecstasy in fragments, the lessons of the
 cardboard cathedrals of the Wasps

 Templar
Never Ones'to keep except in a failbrace like a poem's
    Collisions and collixions   of dirty code

'Pishouge' the casting of the curse   Pithougue the dandy man
     Never make that mistaken agin
Toog an Tooboogie   a fresh saying of no comport except the taste of
 its own wreckish
 seeds
 Pomegranite Barbituate
 Today I made myself Mayour of Merimb ula, tomorrow it shall be

 Broulee

Reify everything   Sparkies!

This is my speech of subtile phlegmata

My speach of subtle spit.

Acknowledgements

Poems in Bunratty were first published in *Jacket2, The Best Australian Poems 2012, Rabbit, Outcrop: Radical Australian Poetry of Land, Cordite Poetry Review, Southerly*, and *A Book of Sea Shantey*.